ACKNOWLEDGMENTS

First and always, I give thanks to God, my healer, my redeemer, and my strength through every storm. Without His love and guidance, this book would not exist.

To every reader holding these pages: thank you for allowing me to share my story with you. My prayer is that God uses these words to bring comfort and healing to your heart.

And to every friend, family member, and faith partner who prayed, encouraged, and believed in the purpose behind this book, thank you. You are part of this testimony.

All glory to God, who makes beauty rise from brokenness.

ABOUT THE AUTHOR

Maryann Heil-Doctor is a faith-based life coach and inspirational writer dedicated to helping others find healing, strength, and divine purpose during life's hardest seasons. Through her personal walk with God, she has discovered that even in life's most painful chapters, including divorce, loss, and transformation, there is always grace waiting to restore the heart. Her mission is to guide others toward spiritual renewal and confidence, reminding each reader that with faith, no season of brokenness is ever wasted.

DIFFERENT ROOTS, SAME REDEEMER

A Grief Coach's Faith Journey to Break Generational Pain and Find Freedom Across Every Culture
Workbook

By COACH MARYANN HEIL-DOCTOR
Friend of Jesus

ISBN

Paperback: 978-1-971141-21-3

Hardcover: 978-1-971141-22-0

Published by: Columbus Book Publishers

www.columbusbookpublishers.com

Printed in the United States of America

TABLE OF CONTENTS

CHAPTER ONE

Breaking Ground — Discovering The Root Cause

BREAKING GROUND IN THE HEART

Every generational cycle begins somewhere. Trauma, beliefs, dysfunction, and patterns rarely start with us, they are inherited, absorbed, or learned through the people and environments that shaped us.

Before healing can begin, you must break the ground of your heart and examine what has been buried there:

- What did your parents model for you?

- What did you normalize because you saw it all your life?

- What patterns did you inherit without realizing it?

- What pain did you absorb because it lived inside your home?

This chapter leads you into gentle excavation, revealing the origin point—the "root cause"—of the patterns you are breaking today.

Generational roots may include:

- Emotional neglect

- Abuse

- Silence around pain

- Addiction cycles

- Poverty thinking

- Abandonment or instability

- Racial or cultural pressures

- Family trauma never addressed

The goal is not to blame, it is to find the root so you can pull it out.

Because what is exposed can be healed.

What is acknowledged can be broken.

What is surrendered can be redeemed.

And Jesus is the Master Gardener.

He uproots what wounded you, and plants what will restore you. This chapter is your beginning, your moment of holy ground-breaking.

WORKSHEET: ROOT REVELATION MAPPING

Fill in each section honestly:

1· Patterns I saw growing up:

_____

2· Pain that still affects me today:

_____

3· Behaviors or beliefs that were "normal," but unhealthy:

_____

4· What I never received emotionally:

_____

5· The first moment I realized something was "wrong" in my family line:

_____

20 MULTIPLE-CHOICE QUESTIONS

1. What is the primary goal of "breaking ground" in generational healing?

A. To blame your parents

B. To uncover the root cause of cycles

C. To focus only on childhood memories

D. To avoid responsibility

Answer:

Because healing begins with identifying the origin.

2. Generational roots often form through:

A. Perfect families

B. Repeated learned behaviors

C. Random events

D. Spiritual gifts

Answer:

3. One major sign of a generational pattern is:

A. A problem appearing only once

B. A repeated cycle across multiple family members

C. A friend mentioning it

D. A dream about your past

Answer:

4. The term "root cause" refers to:

A. The thing you dislike most

B. The emotional source of today's struggles

C. A temporary circumstance

D. A random habit

Answer:

5. Which is an example of an inherited belief?

A. "Money flows easily."

B. "I must never rest."

C. "I love waking up early."

D. "I enjoy learning."

Answer:

6. Trauma can be passed down through:

A. Genetics, behavior, and environment

B. Fashion choices

C. Diet

D. Hairstyles

Answer:

7. Breaking ground requires:

A. Avoidance

B. Honesty

C. Pretending

D. Isolation

Answer:

8. A generational pattern becomes dangerous when:

A. It is ignored

B. It is addressed

C. It is forgiven

D. It is healed

Answer:

9. Jesus is described as the Master Gardener because:

A. He likes plants

B. He uproots what harms and plants what heals

C. He farmed in Scripture

D. He taught botany

Answer:

10. Emotional neglect is best described as:

A. Too many hugs

B. A lack of emotional presence

C. Overfeeding

D. Giving compliments

Answer:

11. Breaking ground helps you:

A. Hide memories

B. Understand your emotional blueprint

C. Become perfect

D. Forget everything

Answer:

12. A root cause is often formed:

A. Suddenly

B. Over years or generations

C. After a vacation

D. During a holiday

Answer:

13. Cultural expectations can shape:

A. Your height

B. Your identity beliefs

C. Your blood type

D. Your allergies

Answer:

14. Pain that is buried often becomes:

A. Empowerment

B. Repetition

C. Celebration

D. Humor

Answer:

15. The first step to generational healing is:

A. Silence

B. Awareness

C. Avoidance

D. Denial

Answer:

16. A repeated emotional response such as anger or fear may indicate:

A. A coincidence

B. A root issue

C. A personality flaw

D. A trend

Answer:

17. "Breaking ground" symbolizes:

A. Making a garden

B. Opening the heart for healing

C. Planting flowers

D. Cleaning your house

Answer:

18. Generational beliefs often influence:

A. Your hair color

B. Your self-worth

C. Your shoe size

D. Your favorite foods

Answer:

19. Jesus heals generational wounds by:

A. Ignoring them

B. Revealing, uprooting, restoring

C. Punishing the family

D. Erasing memories

Answer:

20. The purpose of this chapter is to help you:

A. Avoid emotions

B. Discover the root cause of your struggles

C. Judge your family

D. Become independent

Answer:

8 DECLARATIONS

1. I am courageous enough to examine my roots.

2. What was hidden is now revealed for my healing.

3. I break agreement with every generational lie.

4. I uproot cycles through the power of Jesus Christ.

5. My family's patterns will not dictate my destiny.

6. I receive clarity, truth, and insight from the Holy Spirit.

7. I am the cycle-breaker in my bloodline.

8. What begins with me transforms my generations.

PRAYER

Father, reveal the root of everything that has wounded my heart. Show me the truth, expose what was hidden, and give me courage to face the deep places. Break the ground of my heart gently, and heal every root that has caused pain. Make me the one who uproots cycles for my entire bloodline.

In Jesus' Name, Amen.

10 JOURNAL PROMPTS

1. What patterns do I see repeating in my family?

2. How did these patterns shape me emotionally?

3. Which parts of my upbringing still affect me today?

4. What pain have I avoided confronting?

5. What beliefs did I inherit that were unhealthy?

6. What roots do I feel the Holy Spirit revealing now?

7. What do I wish someone told me when I was young?

8. What moment first made me aware something was wrong?

9. How have I repeated cycles without meaning to?

10. What root do I want God to heal first?

PRACTICAL APPLICATION EXERCISE —

"ROOT DIGGING"

Complete the following sentence:

"I now realize the root of _____ in my life began when _____."

This exercise begins your transformation.

CHAPTER TWO

The Soil We Grew In: How Culture & Family Shape Our Roots

This chapter explores how our family environment, culture, traditions, expectations, and unspoken rules shape our emotional and spiritual development.

Let's begin.

TEACHING SECTION — The Soil That Shaped Your Soul

Every tree grows according to the soil it is planted in. Likewise, every person grows according to the environment that formed them.

Your "soil" includes:

- Your family dynamics

- *Your culture and ethnicity*

- *Your neighborhood*

- *Your early experiences*

- *Your upbringing rules*

- *Emotional expectations*

- *Economic background*

- *Spiritual atmosphere*

Culture plays a powerful role in identity, not just race, but family culture:

- *Some cultures avoid emotions.*

- *Some glorify strength and silence.*

- *Some normalize dysfunction as survival.*

- *Some suppress individuality.*

- *Some value achievement over mental health.*

- *Some confuse loyalty with bondage.*

All of these shape the "soil" you grew in.

But here's the truth:

! The soil you grew in explains you, but it does NOT define your destiny.

Some family soils are:

- Rocky

- Dry

- Toxic

- Chaotic

- Unpredictable

- Overly Strict

- Emotionally Closed

- Shame-Based

- Fear-Controlled

Others may seem healthy but are spiritually shallow.

Regardless of what your soil lacked, Jesus can replant you.

He uproots you from generational soil and places you in:

- Love

- Truth

- Identity

- Healing

- Spiritual Fruitfulness

The purpose of this chapter is to examine:

☞ Where your soil helped you

☞ Where it harmed you

☞ Where it limited you

☞ Where it shaped your emotional survival

☞ Where it formed your identity falsely

You cannot change the soil you were planted in, but you CAN change the soil your future grows from.

WORKSHEET — FAMILY CULTURE ANALYSIS

1· In my family, emotions were:

- Encouraged

- Ignored

- Forbidden

- Punished

- Only expressed in anger

- Expressed in silence

2· My childhood home felt:

- Safe

- Unpredictable

- Fear-driven

- Tense

- Loving

- Lonely

3. In my family, success was defined by:

_____

4. Mistakes were handled by:

_____

5. I learned to survive by:

_____

6. The soil I grew in taught me to believe:

_____

20 MULTIPLE-CHOICE QUESTIONS

1· "Soil" in this chapter refers to:

A· Dirt

B· The environment we were raised in

C· Gardening techniques

D· Family recipes

Answer:

2· Culture influences:

A· Shoe size

B· Emotional expression

C· Height

D· Blood type

Answer:

3· Family culture includes:

A· Holidays only

B. Emotional norms, rules, behaviors

C. TV shows

D. Pets

Answer:

4. A shame-based culture often teaches:

A. Freedom

B. Silence

C. Celebration

D. Transparency

Answer:

5. A fear-controlled home may produce:

A. Emotional security

B. Anxiety

C. Confidence

D. Creativity

Answer:

6. Soil shapes:

A. Identity

B. Eye color

C. Genetics

D. Fashion sense

Answer:

7. Changing your soil means:

A. Moving houses

B. Changing your inner belief system

C. Planting flowers

D. Learning gardening

Answer:

8. Toxic soil creates:

A. Strong roots

B. Shallow or damaged roots

C. Financial success

D· Athletic talent

Answer:

9· Cultural rules that forbid emotions often produce:

A· Openness

B· Suppression

C· Joy

D· Peace

Answer:

10· A chaotic home can foster:

A· Stability

B· Survival mode

C· Predictability

D· Relaxation

Answer:

11· Family expectations can:

A· Determine destiny

B. Influence behavior and identity

C. Control genetics

D. Make you taller

Answer:

12. The soil you grew in explains you, but...

A. It defines your future

B. It limits your destiny

C. It does not determine your destiny

D. It controls everything

Answer:

13. Jesus re-plants us into:

A. Trauma

B. Love and truth

C. Culture

D. Silence

Answer:

14. Toxic soil often creates:

A. Emotional openness

B. Instability

C. Freedom

D. Health

Answer:

15. Understanding your soil helps you:

A. Blame others

B. See why you developed certain patterns

C. Become perfect

D. Avoid healing

Answer:

16. Family silence often teaches:

A. Expression

B. Emotional hiding

C. Confidence

D. Freedom

Answer:

17. Cultural pressure may create:

A. Identity clarity

B. Identity confusion

C. Peace

D. Relaxation

Answer:

18. Replanting spiritually means:

A. Ignoring your past

B. Allowing God to transform your inner foundation

C. Moving cities

D. Changing your last name

Answer:

19. Children raised in fear often become:

A. Bold

B. Anxiety-driven adults

C. Carefree

D. Overconfident

Answer:

20. This chapter helps readers:

A. Judge their family

B. Understand the soil they grew in

C. Avoid change

D. Stay silent

Answer

8 DECLARATIONS

1. I acknowledge the soil that shaped me, but it will not define me.

2. I break agreement with every cultural lie that limited my identity.

3. God is replanting me in healthy, life-giving soil.

4. I release survival mode and step into emotional freedom.

5. My past environment will not restrict my future.

6. The Holy Spirit renews the foundation of my life.

7. My roots will grow in truth, love, and wholeness.

8. I am being replanted for generational blessing.

PRAYER

Lord, reveal the soil that shaped my heart. Show me where it harmed me, where it helped me, and where I need healing. Uproot every lie, fear, or limitation that came from my family or culture. Replant me in Your love, identity, and truth. Restore my foundation and reset my roots.

In Jesus' Name, Amen.

10 JOURNAL PROMPTS

1. What emotions were encouraged or discouraged growing up?

2. What was the atmosphere of my childhood home?

3. How did my family handle conflict?

4. What cultural expectations shaped me?

5. What beliefs did I adopt that weren't healthy?

6. What soil created the biggest wound in my identity?

7. What strengths came from my upbringing?

8. What survival habits do I still use today?

9. What parts of my soil am I ready to release?

10. What new soil do I want God to replant me in?

PRACTICAL APPLICATION EXERCISE —

"Soil Swap"

Complete this statement:

"I am choosing to leave behind _____ so I can grow

in _____."

This is your first step toward replanting.

CHAPTER THREE

The Hidden Entanglements: Soul Ties, Trauma Bonds & Emotional Yokes

TEACHING SECTION — What Holds You When You Don't Even Realize It

Some roots are visible.

Others live underground.

Soul ties, trauma bonds, emotional attachments, and spiritual entanglements are the invisible ropes that keep us tied to pain, people, or past experiences long after the moment has passed.

These ties come from:

- Deep emotional connection

- Abuse cycles

- Toxic relationships

- Inner vows

- Repeated trauma

- Sexual intimacy

- Childhood wounds

- Betrayal or rejection

- Unresolved grief

Many people think soul ties only come from romantic relationships but emotional attachments form ANY time your spirit bonds with someone for survival, identity, or validation.

A soul tie becomes unhealthy when you feel:

- Drained instead of strengthened

- Dependent instead of supported

- Guilty for setting boundaries

- Afraid to leave

- Tied to memories that still hurt

- Unable to heal because a part of you is still attached

Trauma bonds are even deeper·

They form when:

- Love and pain mix

- Abuse and apology cycle

- You cling to someone because leaving feels dangerous

- Your body thinks chaos is normal

- You mistake survival chemistry for love

These bonds are spiritual roots masquerading as emotional connections· But Jesus breaks every chain, including invisible ones·

You cannot walk into freedom still tied to what wounded you·

This chapter reveals the hidden entanglements and leads

you into separation, clarity, release, and healing.

WORKSHEET — IDENTIFYING ENTANGLEMENTS

Check any that apply:

1. In the past, I stayed connected to someone because I feared being alone.

- Yes

- No

2. I struggle to stop thinking about someone who hurt me.

- Yes

- No

3. I feel emotionally responsible for people who drain me.

- Yes

- No

4. When someone disrespects me, I still feel afraid to leave.

- Yes

- No

5. I feel bonded to someone who is no longer in my life.

- Yes

- No

6. My body reacts (anxiety, tension) when I remember certain people.

- Yes

- No

7. I have forgiven someone, but the emotional tie still feels alive.

- Yes

- No

These answers reveal soul tie strength, emotional

attachment patterns, and areas of trauma connection.

20 MULTIPLE-CHOICE QUESTIONS

1. A soul tie forms when:

A. You shake hands

B. Your spirit bonds emotionally, physically, or spiritually

C. You meet someone once

D. You dislike a person

Answer:

2. A trauma bond often includes:

A. Consistent safety

B. A cycle of harm and apology

C. Peaceful communication

D. No emotional attachment

Answer:

3. A sign of an unhealthy soul tie is:

A. Feeling empowered

B. Feeling guilty for having boundaries

C. Feeling free

D. Feeling emotionally detached

Answer:

4. Trauma bonds are dangerous because:

A. They are calm

B. They justify abuse

C. They encourage independence

D. They inspire confidence

Answer:

5. A person with a trauma bond may feel:

A. Free to leave

B. Afraid to leave

C. Indifferent

D. Emotionally stable

Answer:

6. Soul ties can be formed through:

A. Repeated emotional connection

B. Watching TV

C. Eating together once

D. Wearing matching colors

Answer:

7. A healthy soul tie produces:

A. Manipulation

B. Accountability and support

C. Fear

D. Shame

Answer:

8. A trauma bond creates:

A. Clarity

B. Confusion

C. Boundaries

D. Growth

Answer:

9. Jesus breaks soul ties by:

A. Forcing you

B. Healing the root wound

C. Ignoring your pain

D. Minimizing your experience

Answer:

10. The hardest part of soul-tie breaking is:

A. Naming the attachment

B. Buying new clothes

C. Moving houses

D. Changing your number

Answer:

11· Emotional entanglements often begin when:

A· You dislike someone

B· You depend on someone for survival or identity

C· You say no

D· You set boundaries

Answer:

12· Memories that still trigger anxiety may indicate:

A· Growth

B· A lingering soul tie

C· Joy

D· Peace

Answer:

13· Trauma bonds often feel like:

A· Freedom

B. Confusion mixed with emotional attachment

C. Safety

D. Clarity

Answer:

14. An unhealthy tie drains your:

A. Purpose

B. Battery

C. Calendar

D. Electricity

Answer:

15. Breaking soul ties requires:

A. Avoiding emotions

B. Acknowledgment, prayer, and boundaries

C. Denial

D. Silence

Answer:

16· Emotional guilt after leaving a toxic relationship may indicate:

A· A healthy bond

B· A remaining soul tie

C· Victory

D· Closure

Answer:

17· Trauma bonds often disguise themselves as:

A· Peace

B· Passion or "connection"

C· Safety

D· Happiness

Answer:

18. Soul ties can keep you connected to:

A. Only romantic partners

B. Anyone who shaped you deeply

C. Strangers

D. Pets

Answer:

19. Jesus heals entanglements through:

A. Revelation and truth

B. Avoidance

C. Shame

D. Confusion

Answer:

20. The purpose of this chapter is to help you:

A. Enter new trauma

B. Identify hidden emotional bonds

C. Ignore your past

D. Hold onto unhealthy ties

Answer:

8 DECLARATIONS

1. Every unhealthy soul tie in my life is broken in Jesus' name.

2. I detach from every emotional chain that has held me captive.

3. I release every trauma bond that shaped my identity.

4. My spirit is free from every invisible entanglement.

5. I reclaim the pieces of my heart I gave away.

6. Jesus restores my soul to wholeness.

7. I am not tied to my past—I am anchored in Christ.

8. My freedom begins now and continues for generations.

PRAYER

Jesus, reveal every soul tie, every trauma bond, and every hidden entanglement still operating in my heart. Shine Your light on what has kept me emotionally connected to pain. Give me the strength to release every unhealthy attachment, and break every chain that was never meant to hold me. Restore every fractured place within me.

In Your Name, Amen.

10 JOURNAL PROMPTS

1. Who have I felt emotionally tied to long after the relationship ended?

2. What memories still trigger emotional reactions in me?

3. What patterns do I repeat because of emotional attachment?

4. What parts of my identity came from unhealthy connections?

5. When did I first feel "bonded" to someone who hurt me?

6. What ties do I feel the Holy Spirit revealing now?

7. What beliefs came from trauma instead of truth?

8. What boundary have I been afraid to set?

9. What emotional pieces of myself do I want to reclaim?

10. What would freedom from these ties feel like?

PRACTICAL APPLICATION EXERCISE —

"Soul Tie Release Statement"

Write this out:

"I release myself from the emotional, spiritual, and mental connection to _____. I detach every piece of my heart that was tied to this person or experience. I am whole, I am free, I am restored."

CHAPTER FOUR

The Cycles We Repeat: Identifying And Breaking Generational Patterns

TEACHING SECTION — When Life Begins to Look Familiar

Some behaviors are chosen.

Others repeat themselves automatically because they were planted in us long before we had language for them.

A cycle is a repeated pattern of:

- Behavior

- Emotion

- Reaction

- Decision

- Relationship Pattern

- *Coping Mechanism*

- *Avoidance*

- *Pain Response*

Cycles become generational when:

- *You repeat what your parents repeated*

- *You respond how they responded*

- *You carry what they carried*

- *You fear what they feared*

- *You love the way they loved*

- *You shut down the way they shut down*

And here's the truth:

! Cycles repeat until someone recognizes them and breaks them.

In many families, the same patterns show up:

- *Cycles of broken relationships*

- *Cycles of anger and harsh communication*

- *Cycles of addiction*

- *Cycles of poverty mindset*

- *Cycles of mental health struggles*

- *Cycles of silence and emotional avoidance*

- *Cycles of codependency*

- *Cycles of passive suffering*

Cycles of performance-based identity

You do not break a cycle by willpower.

You break it by revelation, intention, healing, and spiritual alignment.

When you understand the cycle, you can interrupt it.

When you interrupt it, you can dismantle it.

When you dismantle it, you can choose differently.

When you choose differently, the next generation inherits healing instead of brokenness.

This chapter helps you see what keeps repeating so you can stop the repetition.

WORKSHEET — CYCLE IDENTIFICATION

1· What emotional reactions repeat often in your life?

(Example: shutting down, lashing out, withdrawing)

2· What patterns do you see in your parents, grandparents, or siblings that also appear in you?

3· What behaviors do you regret but continue repeating anyway?

4· When do these cycles usually appear?

- Stress

- Conflict

- Rejection

- Fear

- Overthinking

- Loneliness

5. What cycle is God showing you in this season?

---

20 MULTIPLE-CHOICE QUESTIONS + ANSWERS

1. A generational cycle is:

A. A single event

B. A repeated pattern across family members

C. A personal preference

D. A random coincidence

Answer:

2. Cycles repeat until:

A. Someone recognizes and disrupts them

B. People ignore them

C. The family grows

D. Time passes

Answer:

3. A cycle can be emotional when it involves:

A. Clothing

B. Repeated ways of reacting

C. Food

D. Holidays

Answer:

4. Harsh communication passed down generations is a sign of:

A. Cooking habits

B. Learned relational patterns

C. Talent

D. Genetics

Answer:

5. A poverty mindset often comes from:

A. Lack of intelligence

B. Generational belief systems

C. Shoe size

D. Personality type

Answer:

6. Emotional avoidance is often learned by:

A. Imitating caregivers

B. Watching TV

C. Reading books

D. Going on vacation

Answer:

7. Cycles continue when:

A. They are acknowledged

B. They remain hidden

C. They are healed

D. They are prayed for

Answer:

8. Breakthrough begins with:

A. Denial

B. Awareness

C. Shame

D. Isolation

Answer:

9. A cycle becomes generational when:

A. It's written down

B. Multiple family members repeat it

C. It happens once

D. It involves a career

Answer:

10. You disrupt a cycle by:

A. Doing nothing

B. Choosing differently

C. Blaming others

D. Running away

Answer:

11. Repeated unhealthy relationships often indicate:

A. Good luck

B. A relational cycle

C. A new beginning

D. Maturity

Answer:

12. Jesus breaks generational cycles through:

A. Minimizing behavior

B. Healing the root cause

C. Ignoring the issue

D. Avoiding conflict

Answer:

13. A cycle of fear may produce:

A. Boldness

B. Overthinking and paralysis

C. Clarity

D. Confidence

Answer:

14. Cycles thrive in:

A. Silence

B. Accountability

C. Boundaries

D. Wisdom

Answer:

15. A repeated emotional trigger may indicate:

A. Growth

B. A cycle acting out

C. Victory

D. Peace

Answer:

16. Addiction cycles often begin with:

A. Emotional pain

B. Boredom

C. Celebration

D. Friendship

Answer:

17. The enemy uses cycles to:

A. Strengthen you

B. Trap generations

C. Clarify identity

D. Build confidence

Answer:

18. Boundaries break cycles by:

A. Angering others

B. Protecting your healing

C. Making you selfish

D. Punishing your family

Answer:

19. Awareness without action leads to:

A. Transformation

B. Continued cycles

C. Healing

D. Wisdom

Answer:

20. This chapter teaches you to:

A. Hide patterns

B. Identify and break them

C. Repeat them

D. Accept them

Answer:

8 DECLARATIONS

1. I see the cycles clearly, and clarity is my breakthrough.

2. I am the one chosen to break what broke generations before me.

3. Every generational pattern ends with me.

4. I choose differently, think differently, and live differently.

5. My future is not controlled by my past.

6. I receive divine wisdom to dismantle every cycle.

7. I walk in generational freedom and purpose.

8. My children and their children will inherit healing—not pain.

PRAYER

Father, reveal every hidden cycle in my life. Show me the patterns that repeat and the roots behind them. Give me divine insight to break what has been passed down through generations. Strengthen me to choose differently, think differently, and walk in freedom. Let healing flow through me into every generation after me.

In Jesus' Name, Amen.

10 JOURNAL PROMPTS

1· What cycle do I see clearly in my family line?How has this cycle shown up in my own life?

2· What emotions trigger this cycle?

3· Who modeled this cycle for me growing up?

4· What part of me still benefits from the cycle?

5· What part of me wants to break free?

6· What truth from God confronts this pattern?

7· What boundaries do I need to set to interrupt it?

8· What new behavior will replace the old one?

9· What cycle do I declare broken today?

PRACTICAL APPLICATION — THE CYCLE BREAKER STATEMENT

Complete this and say it out loud:

"The cycle of _____ ends with me. I will not repeat what wounded me. I choose healing, wisdom, and freedom for myself and my generations."

CHAPTER FIVE

Who Am I? Restoring Identity After Broken Roots

TEACHING SECTION — Reclaiming the Self That Trauma Tried to Erase

Identity is the first thing the enemy attacks.

If he can distort your identity, he can distort your decisions,

your relationships, your purpose, your self-worth, and even your view of God.

Many of us inherited identity wounds from:

- Rejection

- Abandonment

- Emotional Neglect

- *Being Compared*

- *Being Overlooked*

- *Being Shamed*

- *Being Silenced*

- *Trauma*

- *Criticism*

- *Perfectionism*

- *Cultural Pressure*

- *Family Expectations*

Identity was shaped long before you understood you had one.

Trauma doesn't just wound you —

it rewrites who you think you are.

You begin to say things like:

- *"I'm not enough."*

- *"I'm too much."*

- *"I'm a burden."*

- *"I can't trust anyone."*

- *"I don't deserve good relationships."*

- *"I'm invisible."*

- *"I'm just like my family."*

- *"I'll always struggle."*

These are not truths.

These are identity lies.

Healing requires identity replacement:

☞ *Reject the lie*

☞ *Reveal the truth*

☞ *Reinforce the truth*

☞ *Rebuild identity around Christ, not trauma*

This chapter helps you uproot the false labels trauma gave you and reclaim the identity God originally assigned you.

WORKSHEET — IDENTITY LIE VS. IDENTITY TRUTH

Write down the lie trauma taught you:

_____

Now rewrite it with God's truth:

_____

What label did your family put on you?

_____

What label does God place on you instead?

_____

Who were you trying to be in order to receive love?

_____

Who does Jesus say you already are?

_____

20 MULTIPLE-CHOICE QUESTIONS + ANSWERS

1. Identity is often shaped during:

A. Adulthood

B. Childhood

C. Retirement

D. Vacations

Answer:

2. Trauma affects identity by:

A. Strengthening your self-worth

B. Distorting your beliefs about yourself

C. Making you taller

D. Improving self-esteem

Answer:

3. Identity lies come from:

A. God

B. Painful experiences and false beliefs

C. Healthy environments

D. Encouragement

Answer:

4. The enemy's first attack is often on:

A. Your hobbies

B. Your identity

C. Your wardrobe

D. Your social media

Answer:

5. Identity wounds come from:

A. Rejection or neglect

B. Winning an award

C. Getting a new job

D. A birthday party

Answer:

6. One sign of identity distortion is:

A. Confidence

B. Believing you're not enough

C. Healthy boundaries

D. Clear purpose

Answer:

7. Identity replacement requires:

A. Denial

B. Truth

C. Avoidance

D. Shame

Answer:

8. **A person shaped by criticism may become:**

A. Bold

B. Fearful and performance-driven

C. Joyful

D. Indifferent

Answer:

9. **When Jesus restores identity, He:**

A. Confirms the lie

B. Rewrites your truth

C. Minimizes your worth

D. Complicates your life

Answer:

10. **Cultural pressure can distort identity by:**

A. Encouraging authenticity

B. Expecting perfection or conformity

C. Building confidence

D. Affirming individuality

Answer:

11. Identity in Christ is based on:

A. Flaws

B. Trauma

C. Truth and purpose

D. Family tradition

Answer:

12. A healthy identity produces:

A. Fear

B. Confidence and clarity

C. Confusion

D. Shame

Answer:

13· A false identity often leads to:

A· Free choices

B· Self-sabotage

C· Stability

D· Purpose

Answer:

14· God replaces identities through:

A· His Word

B· Negative thoughts

C· Culture

D· Comparison

Answer:

15· A person with a strong identity in Christ:

A· Accepts mistreatment

B· Sets boundaries confidently

C. Avoids growth

D. Stays silent

Answer:

16. Identity healing begins when you:

A. Hide your feelings

B. Confront your wounds

C. Ignore your past

D. Pretend everything is fine

Answer:

17. True identity is rooted in:

A. Trauma

B. Christ

C. Past mistakes

D. Family pressure

Answer:

18. Identity lies often begin with:

A. Encouragement

B. Wounding words or actions

C. Celebrations

D. Breakthroughs

Answer:

19. You restore identity by:

A. Repeating negative self-talk

B. Replacing old labels with God's truth

C. Staying silent

D. Avoiding growth

Answer:

20. This chapter helps you:

A. Accept false beliefs

B. Restore identity

C. Create new trauma

D. Stay confused

Answer:

8 DECLARATIONS

1. I reject every false identity spoken over me.

2. I embrace who God says I am.

3. My worth is not defined by my wounds.

4. Trauma does not get the final word about me.

5. I walk confidently in my God-given identity.

6. Every false label is broken off my life.

7. I am chosen, seen, loved, and restored.

8. I rise into the fullness of who I was created to be.

PRAYER

Father, reveal every false identity I've carried. Show me where trauma rewrote my truth. Heal the places where rejection, shame, or fear shaped me. Restore my identity in You. Replace every lie with Your Word. Help me walk boldly in who You created me to be.

In Jesus' Name, Amen.

10 JOURNAL PROMPTS

1. What lie about myself have I believed the longest?

2. Where did that lie come from?

3. How has that lie shaped my relationships?

4. What does God say about me instead?

5. What parts of myself did I hide to fit into my family culture?

6. What identity wound still affects me today?

7. What label am I ready to surrender?

8. What truth am I ready to embrace?

9. Who do I become when I believe God's truth?

10. What identity does Jesus want to restore in me today?

PRACTICAL APPLICATION — "MY TRUTH STATEMENT"

Write this out:

"I am not who trauma said I was. I am who God created me to be: healed, whole, chosen, and loved."

Declare it for the next 7 days.

CHAPTER SIX

The Internal Battles: Healing The Mind, Heart & Spirit

TEACHING SECTION — The War Within

Most people think spiritual battles happen "out there," but the greatest war takes place inside us:

- In our thoughts

- In our emotions

- In our reactions

- In our beliefs

- In our identity

- In our private battles

- In the quiet places no one sees

The enemy doesn't need to destroy your life if he can first invade your mind.

The internal battle often consists of:

1. Mental Battles

- Overthinking

- intrusive thoughts

- Fear-based assumptions

- Negative self-talk

- Mental replay of trauma

- Worrying about outcomes

- Expecting hurt

These thoughts become mental "loops" that trap peace.

2. Emotional Battles

- Mood Swing

- Emotional Shutdown

- *Anxiety*

- *Anger*

- *Numbness*

- *Emotional Flashbacks*

- *Shame Spirals*

Emotions are powerful, but unhealed emotions try to rule the heart.

3. **Spiritual Battles**

- *Doubt*

- *Confusion*

- *Hopelessness*

- *Feeling disconnected from God*

- *Spiritual Heaviness*

- *Fatigue*

- *Loss of desire to pray*

Many internal battles started before you had language for them.

Some battles began when trauma taught your mind to survive, not to feel safe.

But here is the truth:

God heals the inside before He transforms the outside

Healing the internal world requires:

replacing thoughts

- Processing Emotions

- Spiritual Renewal

- Inner Honesty

- Grace For Yourself

- Rewiring Belief Systems

- Surrendering Lies For Truth

This chapter teaches you to recognize the war inside you, and how to win it with God's help.

WORKSHEET — MIND, HEART & SPIRIT CHECK-IN

1. My current mental battle is:

_____

2. My recurring emotional struggle is:

_____

3. The lie my mind repeats most is:

_____

4. The truth God wants me to believe is:

_____

5. Spiritually, I feel:

- Connected

- Disconnected

- Confused

- Hungry for God

- Weary

- Hopeful

6. I need God to restore this part of me most:

---

20 MULTIPLE-CHOICE QUESTIONS + ANSWERS

1. The internal battle takes place in:

A. The weather

B. The mind, heart, and spirit

C. Your neighborhood

D. Public places

Answer:

2. Mental battles often include:

A. Physical pain

B. Overthinking and intrusive thoughts

C. Eating habits

D. Fashion

Answer:

3. Emotional battles are typically rooted in:

A. Math

B. Unprocessed feelings

C. Physical exercise

D. Diet

Answer:

4. Spiritual battles may show up as:

A. Joy

B. Confusion or doubt

C. Achievement

D. Strength only

Answer:

5. Unhealed emotions often try to:

A. Protect you

B. Rule your decisions

C. Strengthen your purpose

D. Make you joyful

Answer:

6. Negative thought loops can:

A. Bring peace

B. Drain energy and clarity

C. Cause financial success

D. Increase confidence

Answer:

7. Trauma often teaches the mind to:

A. Feel safe

B. Survive

C. Celebrate

D. Trust easily

Answer:

8. A sign of a spiritual battle is:

A. Feeling energized

B. Feeling disconnected from God

C. Feeling optimistic

D. Feeling creative

Answer:

9. Emotional shutdown is usually caused by:

A. Joy

B. Overwhelm or past wounds

C. Vacation

D. Friendship

Answer:

10. Winning internal battles requires:

A. Denial

B. Awareness and truth

C. Avoiding your emotions

D. Blaming others

Answer:

11. Overthinking is a form of:

A. Stress response

B. Celebration

C. Recreation

D. Spiritual gift

Answer:

12· Internal battles grow stronger when:

A· You face them

B· You ignore them

C· You get support

D· You speak truth

Answer:

13· The enemy targets your mind because:

A· It's fragile

B· It shapes your beliefs and decisions

C· He wants to improve your thoughts

D· He has nothing else to do

Answer:

14· God heals internal battles by:

A· Making you forget

B· Renewing your mind and restoring your heart

C· Punishing you

D· Ignoring your pain

Answer:

15· Emotional flashbacks mean:

A· You want attention

B· Your body remembers pain your mind tried to forget

C· You're dramatic

D· You're weak

Answer:

16· A person battling hopelessness may feel:

A· Motivated

B· Spiritually heavy

C· Excited

D· Energetic

Answer:

17. Replacing lies with truth is part of:

A. Avoidance

B. Identity restoration

C. Shame

D. Emotional shutdown

Answer:

18. Healing internal battles requires:

A. Pretending

B. Processing emotions and renewing thoughts

C. Hiding pain

D. Criticizing yourself

Answer:

19. The purpose of internal healing is to:

A. Make you emotional

B. Build a stable foundation for your future

C· Create more trauma

D· Encourage fear

Answer:

20· This chapter teaches you to:

A· Hide the war within

B· Identify and confront internal battles

C· Accept emotional chaos

D· Ignore triggers

Answer:

8 DECLARATIONS

1. My mind is being renewed by God's truth.

2. My heart is healing from every emotional wound.

3. My spirit is being strengthened daily.

4. I am no longer ruled by old mental patterns.

5. God's peace guards my thoughts and emotions.

6. Every inner battle is turning into inner strength.

7. My thoughts align with heaven's truth.

8. I walk in mental, emotional, and spiritual freedom.

PRAYER

Lord, heal the battles inside me that no one else knows about. Renew my mind with truth. Restore my heart from hidden wounds. Strengthen my spirit where it has grown weary. Break every lie, silence every tormenting thought, and breathe peace over my inner world.

In Jesus' Name, Amen.

10 JOURNAL PROMPTS

1. What internal battle do I fight most often?

2. What lie does the enemy whisper to me?

3. What truth does God speak over me?

4. When do my emotions feel most overwhelming?

5. What triggers my mental battles?

6. How has trauma shaped my inner world?

7. What part of my heart needs healing right now?

8. How does my spirit feel—tired, hungry, hopeful?

9. What thought pattern am I ready to surrender?

10. What does peace look like for me?

PRACTICAL APPLICATION — "THOUGHT REPLACEMENT PRACTICE"

Write this:

Lie: ""

Truth: ""

Say the truth three times each day for 7 days.

CHAPTER SEVEN

The Chains That Bind: Addiction, Escape Patterns & Emotional Numbing

TEACHING SECTION — When Comfort Becomes a Cage

Not all chains are made of metal.

Some are made of habits, coping mechanisms, and emotional escapes we learned to rely on when life became too heavy.

Addictions and escape patterns form when:

- The heart is overwhelmed

- The mind is overloaded

- The emotions are unprocessed

- Trauma is unhealed

- Pain feels too difficult to face

People often think addiction only refers to substances.

But addiction can also be:

- Emotional Escape

- Attaching to toxic relationships

- People-Pleasing

- Overeating

- Overspending

- Social Media Obsession

- Pornography

- Gambling

- Workaholism

- Seeking Validation

- Codependency

- Fantasy Thinking

- *Emotional Detachment*

- *Thrill-Seeking*

- *Perfectionism*

- *Emotional Numbing*

Addiction is anything you turn to for comfort, escape, or survival instead of God.

Addictions grow when pain is silenced.

They become cycles when the behavior temporarily soothes a deeper wound.

Jesus doesn't shame people in bondage —He delivers them.

Healing addiction means:

- *Naming the root pain*

- *Confronting emotional wounds*

- *Breaking spiritual ties*

- Rebuilding coping skills

- Receiving God's empowerment

- Replacing the chain with freedom

This chapter teaches you to recognize the cage, understand its door, and walk out of it.

WORKSHEET — WHAT I RUN TO WHEN I'M HURTING

1. When I feel overwhelmed, I usually turn to...

_____

2. When I feel lonely, I often reach for...

_____

3. When I feel rejected, I try to...

_____

4. When I feel anxious, I tend to...

_____

5. What escape pattern do I feel the Holy Spirit highlighting?

_____

20 MULTIPLE-CHOICE QUESTIONS + ANSWERS

1. Addiction is best described as:

A. A lack of willpower

B. A repeated escape pattern tied to pain

C. A personality trait

D. A hobby

Answer:

2. Emotional numbing happens when:

A. You feel too much joy

B. The heart shuts down to avoid pain

C. You exercise

D. You rest

Answer:

3· Pain that is not processed becomes:

A· Strength

B· Addiction fuel

C· Wisdom

D· Celebration

Answer:

4· Addiction often begins as:

A· A joke

B· A comfort mechanism

C· A healthy hobby

D· A good habit

Answer:

5· Codependency is a form of:

A· Freedom

B· Emotional addiction

C. Budgeting

D. Planning

Answer:

6. A person trying to avoid emotional pain may:

A. Face the truth

B. Escape into distractions

C. Communicate clearly

D. Find peace easily

Answer:

7. Workaholism is:

A. Productivity

B. Using achievement to numb emotional wounds

C. Time management

D. A blessing

Answer:

8. Overspending may be triggered by:

A. Financial wisdom

B. Emotional emptiness

C. Rest

D. Peace

Answer:

9. Pornography addiction is rooted in:

A. Curiosity

B. Emotional disconnection and fantasy escape

C. Television

D. Fashion

Answer:

10. People-pleasing becomes bondage when:

A. You serve others

B. You lose yourself to maintain approval

C. You are kind

D. You volunteer

Answer:

11. Addictions often thrive in:

A. Honesty

B. Secrecy

C. Prayer

D. Healing

Answer:

12. Trauma bonds and addictions both:

A. Strengthen identity

B. Create cycles of dependence

C. Encourage wholeness

D. Build trust

Answer:

13. One sign of addiction is:

A. Healthy boundaries

B. Loss of self-control

C. Joy

D. Confidence

Answer:

14. Healing addiction requires:

A. Isolation

B. Naming the root wound

C. Shame

D. Avoidance

Answer:

15. Many addictions begin because the person is trying to:

A. Celebrate

B. Escape

C. Grow

D. Learn

Answer:

16. Numbing emotions leads to:

A. Emotional maturity

B. Emotional disconnection

C. Wisdom

D. Joy

Answer:

17. Jesus delivers by:

A. Condemning

B. Healing the root pain

C. Ignoring the issue

D. Punishment

Answer:

18. Addictions become stronger when:

A. You confront them

B. You hide them

C. You seek support

D. You pray

Answer:

19. Escaping into fantasy or relationships is often a way to:

A. Grow spiritually

B. Avoid emotional pain

C. Solve problems

D. Celebrate achievements

Answer:

20. This chapter teaches you to:

A. Accept bondage

B. Recognize escape patterns

C. Enter new addictions

D. Stay in cycles

Answer:

8 DECLARATIONS

1. Every chain of addiction in my life is breaking in Jesus' name.

2. I confront pain instead of escaping it.

3. My coping mechanisms no longer control me.

4. I replace every escape pattern with God's truth.

5. I walk in emotional and spiritual freedom.

6. I choose healing over numbing.

7. Every generational addiction ends with me.

8. I am fully delivered, fully free, fully whole.

PRAYER

Father, reveal every escape pattern, addiction, and emotional numbness I've carried. Expose the wounds underneath them. Give me courage to face what I've been avoiding and strength to break every chain that has held me captive. Heal the pain beneath the behavior, and fill every empty place with Your presence.

In Jesus' Name, Amen.

10 JOURNAL PROMPTS

1. What do I run to when I'm hurting?

2. What wound is hiding beneath my addiction or escape pattern?

3. What emotion do I fear feeling the most?

4. What behavior do I want to break free from?

5. What lie does this addiction promise to soothe?

6. When did this pattern begin?

7. What does freedom look like for me?

8. What part of my life is affected the most by this chain?

9. What truth replaces the lie behind the addiction?

10. What step can I take today toward freedom?

PRACTICAL APPLICATION — "BREAKING THE CHAIN" STATEMENT

Write this:

"I break agreement with the addiction of _____. I surrender the root pain behind it, and I choose healing over escape. I am free in Jesus' name."

Repeat daily.

CHAPTER EIGHT

The Silent Suffering: Domestic Abuse, Emotional Safety & Finding Your Voice

TEACHING SECTION — When Love Hurts and Silence Speaks the Loudest

Domestic abuse rarely begins loudly.

Most of the time, it begins quietly — through control, manipulation, subtle disrespect, and emotional imbalance.

It grows stronger through silence and fear.

Abuse can take many forms:

- Emotional

- Verbal

- Physical

- Spiritual

- *Financial*

- *Psychological*

And every form is damaging.

People remain in abusive environments because:

- *They fear retaliation*

- *They fear being alone*

- *They hope the person will change*

- *They were conditioned to endure pain*

- *They were raised in abuse and think it's normal*

- *They believe love and suffering coexist*

- *They feel responsible for the abuser's emotions*

- *They have children*

- *They fear losing financial stability*

- *They have been worn down emotionally*

Here's a truth many never hear:

! Abuse is not your fault.

You did not cause it.

You did not deserve it.

And you are not required by God to stay in it.

Abuse damages the heart first:

- You begin shrinking

- You silence yourself

- You walk on eggshells

- You question your reality

- You stop dreaming

- You forget who you were before the abuse

Many victims experience identity erosion —

a slow loss of self-esteem, confidence, and inner voice.

But here's the hope:

! God restores what abuse tried to erase.

! *He rebuilds your voice, value, and emotional safety.*

! *He brings courage to leave what breaks you.*

! *He heals the wounds no one saw.*

This chapter helps you name what hurt you and reclaim what was stolen.

WORKSHEET — SIGNS OF EMOTIONAL & DOMESTIC ABUSE

Check all that apply — awareness is healing:

1. In my relationship or home, I experienced:

- Fear

- Control

- Manipulation

- Silent treatment

- Explosive anger

- Belittling

- Jealousy or monitoring

- Isolation

- Physical harm

2· I often felt:

- Afraid to speak

- Blamed for everything

- Guilty for having needs

- Emotionally drained

- Invisible

- Used

- Confused

3· I lost these parts of myself:

4· What I wish I could have said but couldn't:

5· The moment I realized this wasn't love:

---

20 MULTIPLE-CHOICE QUESTIONS + ANSWERS

1. Domestic abuse is primarily about:

A. Love

B. Power and control

C. Miscommunication

D. Stress

Answer:

2. Emotional abuse includes:

A. Encouragement

B. Mocking, belittling, and manipulation

C. Healthy correction

D. Silence

Answer:

3. Victims often stay in abusive relationships because:

A. They enjoy it

B. They fear consequences or being alone

C. They love pain

D. They are weak

Answer:

4. Abuse often begins:

A. Loudly

B. Subtly

C. With gifts

D. Randomly

Answer:

5. One sign of emotional abuse is:

A. Mutual respect

B. Walking on eggshells

C. Freedom of expression

D. Peaceful communication

Answer:

6. Gaslighting involves:

A. Making someone doubt their reality

B. Encouragement

C. Affirmation

D. Honesty

Answer:

7. Financial abuse occurs when:

A. Finances are shared

B. One person controls all money to restrict the other

C. A budget is discussed

D. Groceries are purchased

Answer:

8. A victim of abuse may feel:

A. Empowered

B. Confused and fearful

C. Celebrated

D. Free

Answer:

9. God's intention for relationships is:

A. Control

B. Mutual love and respect

C. Fear

D. Manipulation

Answer:

10. Abuse thrives in:

A. Silence

B. Community

C. Counseling

D. Prayer

Answer:

11. Spiritual abuse happens when:

A. A partner prays for you

B. Scripture is used to manipulate or control

C. A couple goes to church

D. Faith is shared

Answer:

12. Physical abuse always includes:

A. Bruises

B. Harm or threat of harm

C. Gifts

D. Apologies

Answer:

13. Emotional safety means:

A. Feeling silenced

B. Feeling free to express yourself without fear

C. Avoiding conversations

D. Hiding emotions

Answer:

14. Verbal abuse may include:

A. Compliments

B. Constant criticism

C. Encouragement

D. Patience

Answer:

15. Children raised in abusive homes:

A. Always grow stronger

B. Often repeat or suffer from the cycle

C. Are unaffected

D. Forget everything

Answer:

16. Healing from abuse requires:

A. Shame

B. Naming the abuse and seeking support

C. Silence

D. Blaming yourself

Answer:

17. God calls His children to:

A. Stay in harm

B. Walk in safety, dignity, and peace

C. Accept mistreatment

D. Endure abuse

Answer:

18. A victim regains their voice by:

A. Staying quiet

B. Speaking truth safely

C. Pleasing the abuser

D. Hiding

Answer:

19. Abuse damages:

A. Identity and self-worth

B. Furniture

C. Clothing

D. Vehicles

Answer:

20. The purpose of this chapter is to:

A. Excuse abuse

B. Help identify abuse and begin healing

C. Create fear

D. Encourage silence

Answer:

8 DECLARATIONS

1. I deserve safety, dignity, and love.

2. I break every emotional and spiritual chain tied to abuse.

3. My voice matters, and I will not be silenced.

4. God is restoring every part of me that abuse tried to erase.

5. I am rising from what tried to destroy me.

6. I walk in courage, clarity, and protection.

7. My heart is healing, and my spirit is strengthening.

8. Abuse ends with me — it will not touch the next generation.

PRAYER

Father, heal the wounds I suffered in silence. Restore my voice, my confidence, and my sense of worth. Break every chain of fear, control, manipulation, and shame. Remove the emotional residue of abuse from my heart. Cover me with Your protection and surround me with Your love. Give me the courage to walk in truth, healing, and emotional safety.

In Jesus' Name, Amen.

10 JOURNAL PROMPTS

1. What form of abuse hurt me the most emotionally?

2. What part of myself did I lose in that environment?

3. What did I wish I could have said?

4. Who did I become in order to survive?

5. What lie did the abuser make me believe?

6. What truth does God speak over that lie?

7. What boundary do I need to honor today?

8. What would emotional safety look like for me?

9. What part of my voice is God restoring?

10. What step toward healing am I ready to take?

PRACTICAL APPLICATION — "RESTORING MY VOICE" EXERCISE

Write this:

"I reclaim my voice, my worth, and my identity. Abuse no longer defines me. God restores what was stolen and heals what was broken."

Say it once a day for the next 7 days.

CHAPTER NINE

Redeemed, Restored & Released: How God Turned My Story Into A Ministry

TEACHING SECTION — When God Steps Into the Ruins

There comes a moment in a person's story when God steps into the ruins — not to judge the broken pieces, but to rebuild what looked impossible to repair.

Your story, Coach, is a testimony of:

- Redemption

- Deliverance

- Breaking Generational Curses

- Healing From Trauma

- Rising From Addiction

- *Escaping Abuse*

- *Reclaiming Identity*

- *Walking into purpose*

This chapter reflects the journey many take:

1. The Breaking Point

Where life becomes so overwhelming that survival replaces living.

Where fear, pain, addiction, trauma, or abuse feel unbearable.

Where you say, "God, if You don't save me, I won't make it."

2. The Divine Intervention

God shows up in ways that don't always look dramatic —

sometimes it's a whisper,

sometimes a moment of clarity,

sometimes a door opening or closing,

sometimes a supernatural shift in your heart.

Grace steps in where strength fails.

3. The Deliverance

Deliverance is not only the removal of a demon —

it is the release of:

- Old Identities

- Soul Ties

- Generational Patterns

- Addictions

- False Beliefs

- Emotional Chains

- Spiritual Heaviness

- Shame

- Fear

Deliverance is God saying,

"You will not live one more day as the version of yourself trauma created."

4. The Restoration

God restores:

- Voice

- Identity

- Confidence

- Emotional Clarity

- Spiritual Authority

- Boundaries

- Self-Worth

- Purpose

- Calling

He not only heals wounds —

He turns them into weapons.

5. The Release Into Purpose

This is where the story becomes a ministry.

What tried to kill you becomes the platform you stand on.

Just like you, Coach:

Friend of Jesus Ministry was birthed from your healing — not your perfection.

Your story teaches others that deliverance is real, healing is possible, and God still rescues His children from generational chains.

WORKSHEET — MY REDEMPTION STORY MAP

1. My breaking point moment:

_____

2. How God stepped in:

_____

3. What I was delivered from:

_____

4. What God restored in me:

_____

5. How my story is helping others:

_____

20 MULTIPLE-CHOICE QUESTIONS + ANSWERS

1. Redemption means:

A. Ignoring the past

B. God transforming what was broken

C. Pretending nothing happened

D. Staying wounded

Answer:

2. Deliverance includes freedom from:

A. Joy

B. Soul ties, addictions, and generational patterns

C. Blessings

D. Encouragement

Answer:

3. God often intervenes:

A. Only when people are perfect

B. At breaking points

C. When we hide from Him

D. On holidays

Answer:

4. Restoration includes:

A. Losing identity

B. Rebuilding voice, confidence, and purpose

C. Becoming weaker

D. Accepting shame

Answer:

5. Shame says:

A. "You are the mistake."

B. "You are healed."

C. "You are chosen."

D. "You are enough."

Answer:

6. Grace says:

A. "Try harder."

B. "You're not alone."

C. "You are perfect without God."

D. "Stay broken."

Answer:

7. A soul tie is:

A. A healthy friendship

B. An unhealthy emotional/spiritual bond

C. A sports activity

D. A work relationship

Answer:

8· Deliverance breaks:

A· Blessings

B· Chains

C· Joy

D· Humor

Answer:

9· God uses your story to:

A· Shame you

B· Empower others

C· Hide you

D· Limit you

Answer:

10· The Friend of Jesus Ministry was birthed from:

A· Perfection

B· Healing and deliverance

C. Giving up

D. Silence

Answer:

11. Restoration reveals:

A. Who trauma made you

B. Who God originally created you to be

C. Who society wants

D. Who your family expects

Answer:

12. Generational curse breaking begins with:

A. Denial

B. Awareness + spiritual intervention

C. Pretending

D. Fear

Answer:

13. Deliverance is a sign of:

A. Weakness

B. God's compassion

C. Punishment

D. Luck

Answer:

14. After deliverance, a person often feels:

A. Empty

B. Lighter, clearer, renewed

C. Confused

D. Afraid

Answer:

15. Purpose is often discovered:

A. Through pain redeemed

B. Randomly

C· In comfort

D· Through perfection

Answer:

16· God turns wounds into:

A· Weapons

B· More wounds

C· Silence

D· Fear

Answer:

17· Ministry is birthed from:

A· Suffering alone

B· Healing shared

C· Gossip

D· Doubt

Answer:

18. Restoration includes reclaiming:

A. Trauma

B. Identity

C. Shame

D. Fear

Answer:

19. God's grace empowers you to:

A. Stay stuck

B. Break cycles

C. Hide your story

D. Repeat patterns

Answer:

20. This chapter teaches you:

A. How to stay in bondage

B. How God redeems your story and calls you into purpose

C. How to erase your past

D. How to avoid healing

Answer:

8 DECLARATIONS

1. God has redeemed my story completely.

2. I am delivered from every chain that once bound me.

3. My voice, identity, and purpose are fully restored.

4. My testimony carries power and authority.

5. My past does not disqualify me — it prepares me.

6. I walk boldly into the calling God has placed on my life.

7. I am chosen to break generational cycles for my family.

8. My ministry is a result of God's grace, not my perfection.

PRAYER

Lord, thank You for redeeming my story. Thank You for delivering me from every chain, every soul tie, every addiction, and every generational pattern. Restore my identity fully, strengthen my voice, and release me into the purpose You created for me. Let my life and testimony bring healing to others. Use my story to grow the Friend of Jesus Ministry and to shine Your glory everywhere I go.

In Jesus' Name, Amen.

10 JOURNAL PROMPTS

1. What moment changed everything for me?

2. How did God deliver me?

3. What part of my story carries the most power?

4. What wound did God heal that I never thought He could?

5. What did God restore in me emotionally?

6. What generational chain broke because of me?

7. What is God calling me to do in ministry?

8. Who needs to hear my testimony?

9. What fear tries to stop me from sharing my story?

10. How will I honor God through my purpose?

PRACTICAL APPLICATION — "MY REDEMPTION STATEMENT"

Write this boldly:

"My story is redeemed. My life is restored. My calling is activated. God turned my pain into purpose, and I will use it to set others free."

Say it for the next 7 mornings.

CHAPTER TEN

Untangling The Soul: Breaking Unhealthy Soul Ties & Reclaiming Your Freedom

TEACHING SECTION — The Invisible Threads That Bind Us

A soul tie is an invisible connection between two people — emotional, spiritual, or physical that can influence your:

- *Thoughts*

- *Decisions*

- *Desires*

- *Identity*

- *Self-Worth*

- *Relationships*

- Emotions

- Spiritual Walk

Soul ties are not always negative.

Healthy soul ties come from God:

- Covenant Marriage

- Deep Friendship

- Family

- God-Ordained Mentorship

- Spiritual Alignment

But unholy soul ties form when relationships are rooted in:

- Trauma

- Manipulation

- Control

- Sexual Sin

- *Abuse*

- *Emotional Dependency*

- *Repeated Breakups*

- *Fear Of Abandonment*

- *Intense, Obsessive Attachment*

- *Toxic Cycles*

Unhealthy soul ties pull you back into patterns you tried to escape.

You feel "attached" even when you want to walk away.

Unholy soul ties often create:

- *Confusion*

- *Emotional Flashbacks*

- *Mental Obsession*

- *Longing For Someone Who Hurt You*

- *Difficulty Moving On*

- Spiritual Heaviness

- Repetitive Dreams

- Craving Closure that never comes

- Replaying Conversations

- Guilt Or Shame

- Inability to release the Past

Some relationships create trauma bonds, where pain and "love" get tangled together, making it hard to distinguish abuse from affection.

But here is the hope:

! Every soul tie that God did not create can be broken

! Everyemotional chain can be severed.

! You can reclaim your heart, mind, and spirit.

Breaking soul ties involves:

- Renouncing emotional agreements

- *Releasing the person spiritually*

- *Forgiving*

- *Healing the wound that attached you*

- *Closing spiritual doorways*

- *Inviting the Holy Spirit into the memory*

- *Reclaiming your identity*

This chapter helps you untangle what's been binding you and step into freedom with clarity and peace.

WORKSHEET — IDENTIFYING SOUL TIES

1. Who comes to mind when you think of emotional entanglement?

2. What emotions rise when you think of this person or relationship?

- Pain

- Confusion

- Longing

- Shame

- Anger

- Fear

- Attachment

3. What made the tie form?

- Sexual connection

- Trauma bond

- Repeated breakup cycles

- Codependency

- Emotional dependence

- Manipulation

- Loneliness

4. What part of me did I lose in that connection?

---

5. What does freedom look like for me?

---

20 MULTIPLE-CHOICE QUESTIONS + ANSWERS

1. A soul tie is:

A. A physical rope

B. An emotional/spiritual connection between people

C. A friendship bracelet

D. A financial agreement

Answer:

2. Healthy soul ties come from:

A. Manipulation

B. God

C. Trauma

D. Abuse

Answer:

3. Unhealthy soul ties form through:

A. Encouragement

B. Toxic relationships and emotional dependency

C. Safe friendships

D. Respect

Answer:

4. A trauma bond includes:

A. Mutual healing

B. Cycles of pain and attachment

C. Healthy communication

D. Peace

Answer:

5. Unholy soul ties often create:

A. Clarity

B. Confusion

C. Freedom

D. Peace

Answer:

6. One sign of a soul tie is:

A. Forgetting the person entirely

B. Feeling emotionally tied even after separation

C. Moving on instantly

D. Not caring

Answer:

7. Soul ties grow stronger through:

A. Boundaries

B. Repeated intimacy and emotional need

C. Prayer

D. Healthy communication

Answer:

8. God desires soul ties that are:

A. Controlling

B. Manipulative

C. Healthy and covenant-aligned

D. Abusive

Answer:

9. An unhealthy soul tie affects:

A. Only your weekends

B. Your mind, emotions, and spiritual clarity

C. Your shoes

D. The weather

Answer:

10. Breaking a soul tie requires:

A. Shame

B. Honesty, forgiveness, and spiritual surrender

C. Denial

D. Avoiding healing

Answer:

11. Obsession over a person may indicate:

A. Love

B. A soul tie

C. Peace

D. Strength

Answer:

12. An unhealthy soul tie can feel like:

A. A prison

B. A celebration

C. A vacation

D. A blessing

Answer:

13. Sexual intimacy can form:

A. No emotional connection

B. Deep soul ties

C. A legal contract

D. Instant healing

Answer:

14. A person may stay tied because:

A. They're confused emotionally

B. They enjoy pain

C. God commands it

D. They want financial gain

Answer:

15. Breaking soul ties frees you from:

A. Joy

B. Mental and emotional bondage

C. Faith

D. Blessings

Answer:

16. A healed soul tie becomes:

A. Wisdom

B. Shame

C. Confusion

D. A new soul tie

Answer:

17. The Holy Spirit restores:

A. Trauma bonds

B. Emotional clarity

C. Shame cycles

D. Confusion

Answer:

18· Forgiveness in soul tie breaking means:

A· Reconciliation

B· Releasing emotional and spiritual grip

C· Agreeing with the person

D· Staying in bondage

Answer:

19· You reclaim your identity by:

A· Running backward

B· Breaking every false attachment

C· Pleasing others

D· Numbing emotions

Answer:

20· This chapter teaches you to:

A· Stay emotionally tied

B· Break unhealthy alignments

C. Repeat past cycles

D. Strengthen trauma bonds

Answer:

8 DECLARATIONS

1. Every soul tie God did not create is broken off my life.

2. I release every emotional and spiritual attachment that bound me.

3. My heart is no longer entangled — it is free and whole.

4. I reclaim every part of myself I lost in past relationships.

5. I am emotionally, mentally, and spiritually untangled.

6. I am no longer connected to what God has disconnected me from.

7. My identity is rooted in Christ, not in past relationships.

8. I walk in complete emotional and spiritual freedom.

PRAYER

Lord, shine Your light on every soul tie that has kept me bound. Break every connection rooted in trauma, manipulation, shame, fear, or sin. Heal the wounds that made me attach to the wrong people. Restore clarity where there has been confusion. Close every spiritual doorway opened through unhealthy ties. Reclaim my heart, my identity, and my peace. Release me fully into the freedom You designed for me.

In Jesus' Name, Amen.

10 JOURNAL PROMPTS

1. Who do I still feel emotionally tied to?

2. What wound created this connection?

3. What did I lose in that relationship?

4. What lie did that person or tie teach me?

5. What truth does God speak over that lie?

6. What part of me is ready to be restored?

7. What did I hope this relationship would give me?

8. What do I need to surrender to break this tie?

9. What boundary do I need to set moving forward?

10. What does emotional and spiritual freedom mean to me now?

PRACTICAL APPLICATION — "SOUL TIE BREAKING PROCLAMATION"

Speak this aloud:

"I sever every soul tie that God did not form. I renounce emotional attachments, spiritual bonds, and relational chains that kept me tied to my past. I reclaim my heart, my identity, and my freedom. Whom the Son sets free is free indeed."

Say it for the next 7 days.

CHAPTER ELEVEN

Rewriting The Blueprint: Healing From Dysfunctional Parenting Patterns

TEACHING SECTION — When the Blueprint We Inherited Becomes the Blueprint We Recreate

Families are the first teachers.

Before you had language, identity, or emotional understanding, you were already learning:

- How to love

- How to respond

- How to communicate

- How to cope

- How to handle conflict

- How to express anger

- How to trust

- How to value yourself

Dysfunctional parenting does not always look extreme.

Sometimes it looks like:

- Emotional Distance

- Lack of affection

- Unpredictable anger

- Favoritism

- Criticism

- Neglect

- Codependency

- Overprotection

- Absence

- Perfectionism

- Silent Treatment

- Shame-based discipline

- Children raised in dysfunction grow into adults who:

- Feel unsafe expressing emotion

- Become people-pleasers

- Develop attachment wounds

- Form dysfunctional relationships

- Repeat cycles unconsciously

- Lose their voice

- Carry guilt or shame

- Avoid conflict

- Sabotage good relationships

- Internalize blame

Here's the truth:

! Parents cannot give what they never received.

! Dysfunction is learned, and therefore it can be unlearned.

You are not responsible for the pain that shaped you —

but you are empowered to heal it so you don't pass it down.

Healing dysfunctional parenting patterns includes:

- Releasing resentment

- Understanding generational wounds

- Grieving the love you didn't receive

- Learning new emotional skills

- Building healthy communication

- Setting boundaries

- Forgiving without excusing

- Choosing differently for your children

You get to be the one who says: "The dysfunction stops here."

WORKSHEET — MY FAMILY BLUEPRINT

1· The parenting style I grew up with:

_____

2· The emotional environment of my childhood was:

- Warm

- Cold

- Chaotic

- Confusing

- Fearful

- Lonely

- Unpredictable

3· Patterns I inherited from my parents:

_____

4· Patterns I have unintentionally repeated:

_____

5. The parent I want to become (or would have needed):

---

20 MULTIPLE-CHOICE QUESTIONS + ANSWERS

1. Dysfunctional parenting patterns are often:

A. Random

B. Learned behaviors passed down

C. Genetic mutations

D. Financial habits

Answer:

2. A common sign of dysfunctional parenting is:

A. Healthy affection

B. Emotional neglect

C. Clear communication

D. Encouragement

Answer:

3. Children learn how to handle emotions by:

A. Guessing

B. Watching their caregivers

C. TV

D. Friends

Answer:

4. Shame-based parenting teaches children to believe:

A. They are lovable

B. Something is wrong with them

C. Their needs matter

D. They are safe

Answer:

5. Overprotective parenting can create:

A. Independence

B. Fear of decision-making

C. Confidence

D. Leadership skills

Answer:

6. Adults raised in dysfunction often become:

A. Emotionally secure

B. Conflict avoidant

C. Peaceful communicators

D. Trusting

Answer:

7. The silent treatment teaches children that:

A. Communication is safe

B. Expressing needs is dangerous

C. Boundaries are good

D. Emotions are valid

Answer:

8· Parents who lacked affection often:

A· Over-give emotionally

B· Repeat emotional distance

C· Become affectionate instantly

D· Love perfectly

Answer:

9· Healing dysfunctional patterns requires:

A· Blaming parents

B· Awareness and intentional change

C· Ignoring the past

D· Hoping it improves

Answer:

10· A person may repeat what they grew up with because:

A· They want to

B. It feels familiar

C. It is healthy

D. They prefer pain

Answer:

11. Generational dysfunction stops when:

A. You pretend

B. One person chooses healing

C. Everyone agrees

D. Time passes

Answer:

12. A healthy parent-child relationship includes:

A. Fear

B. Manipulation

C. Safety and communication

D. Silence

Answer:

13· Forgiving your parents means:

A· Excusing their behavior

B· Releasing the emotional hold of the past

C· Returning to harmful environments

D· Pretending nothing happened

Answer:

14· Healing includes:

A· Learning new emotional skills

B· Going backward

C· Blaming permanently

D· Hiding pain

Answer:

15· One reason people struggle with intimacy is:

A· Weather

B· Childhood emotional wounds

C· Diet

D· Shoes

Answer:

16· Dysfunction continues when:

A· You face it

B· It stays unspoken

C· You seek support

D· You heal

Answer:

17· Breaking the cycle means:

A· Becoming perfect

B· Choosing healthier patterns

C· Never making mistakes

D· Raising children without discipline

Answer:

18. A child who felt unheard often becomes an adult who:

A. Speaks boldly

B. Silences themselves

C. Trusts easily

D. Loves freely

Answer:

19. Healthy parenting is built on:

A. Fear

B. Consistency, love, and communication

C. Secrecy

D. Perfection

Answer:

20. This chapter teaches you to:

A. Repeat what hurt you

B. Heal inherited patterns

C. Shame your parents

D. Hide dysfunction

Answer:

8 DECLARATIONS

1. I break every dysfunctional pattern passed down to me.

2. I am creating a new emotional blueprint for my family.

3. I release shame and embrace healing.

4. I am capable of healthy, loving relationships.

5. I forgive my parents without repeating their patterns.

6. I choose growth over generational wounds.

7. My future family will inherit healing, not pain.

8. God is rewriting my story and my lineage.

PRAYER

Father, heal the wounds created by dysfunctional parenting. Show me the patterns I inherited and the patterns I repeated. Give me the wisdom to unlearn what harmed me and the strength to build something new for the generations after me. Restore what was broken in my childhood and empower me to walk as the healed parent, mentor, or leader You created me to be.

In Jesus' Name, Amen.

10 JOURNAL PROMPTS

1. What dysfunctional patterns did I grow up with?

2. How did those patterns shape my beliefs about myself?

3. What part of my childhood still affects my adult relationships?

4. What do I wish my parents had given me emotionally?

5. What parenting style did I inherit without meaning to?

6. What am I ready to release?

7. What emotional skill do I want to learn?

8. What does a healed family environment look like for me?

9. What cycle am I committed to breaking?

10. What new blueprint do I want my future generations to inherit?

PRACTICAL APPLICATION — "THE NEW BLUEPRINT DECLARATION"

Write and repeat this:

"I am creating a healed and healthy family line. The dysfunction ends with me, and the blessing begins with me."

Say it every morning for the next 5 days.

CHAPTER TWELVE

Walking In The Royal Bloodline: Embracing Your God-Given Identity & Authority

TEACHING SECTION — You Are Royalty in the Kingdom of God

After overcoming generational curses,

after facing trauma,

after healing wounds,

after breaking soul ties,

after dismantling dysfunction,

after reclaiming your voice,

after rising from abuse, addiction, and spiritual battles ...

... now you step into who you truly are.

Not the version shaped by pain.

Not the version molded by survival.

Not the version defined by trauma.

Not the version created by family patterns.

But the version God always intended.

Scripture tells us:

"You are a chosen generation, a royal priesthood…" — 1 Peter 2:9

Royalty has:

- *Identity*

- *Authority*

- *Inheritance*

- *Access*

- *Boldness*

- *Confidence*

- Purpose

And these are not earned — they are given through Jesus Christ. **Your Royal Bloodline Rewrites the Old Story**

Where your earthly bloodline carried:

- Addiction

- Abuse

- Rejection

- Poverty

- Shame

- Dysfunction

- Broken Identity

Your heavenly bloodline carries:

- Deliverance

- Healing

- Purpose

- Courage

- Authority

- Blessing

- Clarity

- Destiny

You do not walk as a victim.

You walk as a Kingdom Ambassador, carrying the authority of your Father.

This chapter helps you step fully into that identity — healed, whole, bold, and empowered.

WORKSHEET — CLAIMING MY ROYAL IDENTITY

1· The lie I believed about myself:

_____

2· The truth God speaks over me:

_____

3· The old identity I am releasing:

_____

4· The new identity I am embracing:

_____

5· How I will walk differently as a healed child of God:

_____

20 MULTIPLE-CHOICE QUESTIONS + ANSWERS

1· Your royal identity comes from:

A· Family history

B· Christ

C· Achievements

D· Personality

Answer:

2· A royal priesthood means you:

A· Are insignificant

B· Carry spiritual authority

C· Are forgotten

D· Are powerless

Answer:

3· **The enemy attacks identity because:**

A· He likes you

B· He fears who you will become

C· He wants to bless you

D· He is confused

Answer:

4· **Walking in authority requires:**

A· Shame

B· Knowing who you are in Christ

C· Fear

D· Hiding

Answer:

5· **Your heavenly bloodline replaces:**

A· Generational curses

B· Blessings

C. Confidence

D. Wisdom

Answer:

6. Your past no longer defines you because:

A. You forget it

B. God redeemed it

C. You pretend

D. You deny it

Answer:

7. God-given identity produces:

A. Confusion

B. Confidence

C. Shame

D. Fear

Answer:

8· When you walk in purpose, you:

A· Shrink

B· Shine

C· Hide

D· Fear

Answer:

9· The royal bloodline gives you access to:

A· Doubt

B· Spiritual inheritance

C· Nothing new

D· Trauma

Answer:

10· The old self is:

A· Your destiny

B· Who trauma built

C. Who God created

D. Your authority

Answer:

11. A Kingdom Ambassador represents:

A. The world

B. The Kingdom of God

C. The enemy

D. Culture

Answer:

12. Royal identity requires:

A. Pride

B. Humility and confidence in God

C. Shame

D. Fear

Answer:

13. When you embrace who God says you are, you:

A. Retreat

B. Rise

C. Shrink

D. Doubt

Answer:

14. God-given authority helps you:

A. Enter cycles

B. Break cycles

C. Repeat trauma

D. Stay silent

Answer:

15. Your testimony becomes powerful when you:

A. Hide it

B. Share it

C. Forget it

D. Diminish it

Answer:

16. Your spiritual inheritance includes:

A. Bondage

B. Peace, healing, authority, purpose

C. Addiction

D. Shame

Answer:

17. You are no longer defined by:

A. Trauma

B. Christ

C. Pain

D. Fear

Answer:

18. To walk boldly you must:

A. Believe the old labels

B. Believe the identity God gave you

C. Walk backward

D. Avoid healing

Answer:

19. Your new story begins when you:

A. Repeat the old one

B. Accept God's healing and purpose

C. Hide from your past

D. Stay silent

Answer:

20. The purpose of this chapter is to:

A. Confuse your identity

B. Help you walk fully in the royal bloodline

C. Keep you small

D. Reinforce shame

Answer:

8 DECLARATIONS

1. I am a child of the King, chosen and set apart.

2. I walk boldly in my royal identity.

3. My life carries Kingdom authority and purpose.

4. I reject every label that does not come from God.

5. Generational curses are replaced with generational blessings.

6. I rise above fear, shame, and old identities.

7. I walk in confidence, clarity, and purpose.

8. I am part of God's royal bloodline — and I live like it.

PRAYER

Father, thank You for calling me into Your royal bloodline. Thank You for the identity, authority, and inheritance I have through Christ. Help me release every old label and step fully into who You created me to be. Strengthen me to walk boldly, confidently, and purposefully as Your chosen daughter. Let my healed identity transform generations after me.

In Jesus' Name, Amen.

10 JOURNAL PROMPTS

1. What old identity am I finally releasing?

2. What does my royal identity mean to me?

3. What fears kept me from walking boldly?

4. What truth about myself do I now embrace?

5. What does God say about who I am?

6. What inheritance am I claiming through Christ?

7. How will I live differently as a Kingdom Ambassador?

8. What boundaries protect my new identity?

9. What generational blessing begins with me?

10. What purpose is God calling me to walk into now?

PRACTICAL APPLICATION — "ROAYL WALKING DECLARATION"

Speak this every morning:

"I am royalty. I walk with authority. I carry purpose. I am chosen, healed, and sent by God."

SOLUTIONS & EXPLANATIONS

Workbook Answer Section

Friend of Jesus Ministry

By

Maryann Heil-Doctor

CHAPTER 1 — Solutions & Explanations

1. B — Generational patterns repeat across family lines until recognized and broken.

2. A — Awareness is the first required step toward generational healing.

3. C — Trauma often influences behavior more than conscious choice.

4. B — Roots of dysfunction shape identity early in life.

5. A — Emotional wounds often show up physically or behaviorally.

6. D — Healing begins when hidden pain is brought into the light.

7. B — Family patterns affect how individuals respond in adulthood.

8. A — Generational pain operates silently but powerfully.

9. C — Healing requires identifying the root, not the surface behavior.

10. B — God reveals generational issues through self-reflection and prayer.

11. A — Cycles repeat unconsciously until exposed.

12. D — One healed person can shift the entire generational line.

13. B — Trauma doesn't heal with time; it heals with attention and truth.

14. C — Emotional inheritance is just as real as physical inheritance.

15. A — Behavior patterns often come from learned childhood responses.

16. D — Spiritual bondage is broken through truth and deliverance.

17. C — Many adult struggles began in childhood environments.

18. A — Naming a pattern strips it of power.

19. D — God reveals roots so He can heal them.

20. B — The purpose of the chapter is awareness and root-level healing.

CHAPTER 2 — Solutions & Explanations

1. A — Painful experiences shape generational roots.

2. C — Healing requires looking at the origin story honestly.

3. B — Children absorb emotional patterns before understanding them.

4. D — Trauma alters attachment, trust, and identity.

5. A — Repeating cycles is often unconscious, not intentional.

6. B — Emotional triggers point to unhealed roots.

7. C — God heals from the inside out.

8. A — Breaking curses begins with interrupting inherited patterns.

9. D — Pain passed down becomes generational until confronted.

10. B — Family silence strengthens generational trauma.

11. C — Revealing truth destroys secrecy-based cycles.

12. A — Generational patterns manifest emotionally and spiritually.

13·B — A root problem cannot be solved with surface solutions·

14·C — Identity is shaped by early relationships·

15·A — Trauma-based beliefs attach deeply·

16·B — Pain that is not processed becomes a cycle·

17·D — God exposes roots for transformation·

18·C — Healing reconnects you to your true identity·

19·A — The Holy Spirit guides the uprooting process·

20· B — This chapter teaches root recognition and healing·

CHAPTER 3 — Solutions & Explanations

1· C — Many emotional wounds begin in childhood environments·

2· B — Unmet needs often manifest as adult struggles·

3· A — Childhood pain shapes adult behavior and coping·

4· D — Internal wounds create external patterns·

5. C — Trauma creates survival identities.

6. A — Inner child work addresses foundational pain.

7. B — Rejection wounds form early and shape attachment.

8. C — Your younger self learned patterns you now carry.

9. A — God heals from the earliest wounds outward.

10. D — Restoration includes every version of you.

11. B — Healing the inner child changes adult behavior.

12. A — Emotional triggers often connect to childhood memory.

13. C — Many adult beliefs were formed subconsciously.

14. B — God restores innocence and identity.

15. D — Emotional safety was often missing in early environments.

16. A — Healing childhood wounds frees your adult self.

17. B — Your story makes sense when the root is revealed.

18. C — Identity reconstruction begins in the heart.

19. A — The Holy Spirit comforts your wounded parts.

20. D — The chapter teaches healing from childhood-origin pain.

CHAPTER 4 — Solutions & Explanations

1. B — Cycles repeat until someone recognizes them.

2. A — Recognition interrupts generational repetition.

3. B — Emotional patterns repeat across generations.

4. B — Learned communication becomes a cycle.

5. B — Mindset is inherited emotionally.

6. A — Caregivers model emotion management.

7. B — Hidden patterns repeat by default.

8. B — Awareness is the beginning of breakthrough.

9. B — Repetition across generations defines a cycle.

10. B — New choices break old patterns.

11. B — Relational cycles form from emotional wounds.

12. B — Jesus heals root causes, not symptoms.

13. B — Fear cycles impact decision-making.

14. A — Silence strengthens dysfunction.

15. B — Emotional triggers reflect active cycles.

16. A — Trauma roots fuel addiction cycles.

17. B — The enemy traps families in repetition.

18. B — Boundaries disrupt unhealthy cycles.

19. B — Knowledge without action reinforces cycles.

20. B — The chapter teaches identification and cycle-breaking.

CHAPTER 5 — Solutions & Explanations

1. B — Identity forms in childhood.

2. B — Trauma distorts identity.

3. B — Lies form from wounds.

4. B — The enemy targets identity first.

5. A — Rejection wounds shape beliefs.

6. B — "Not enough" is an identity wound.

7. B — Identity truth replaces identity lies.

8. B — Performance-based identity comes from criticism.

9. B — Jesus restores truth-based identity.

10. B — Culture pressures create false identities.

11. C — Identity in Christ is built on truth.

12. B — Healthy identity produces confidence.

13. B — False identity leads to self-sabotage.

14. A — The Word rewrites identity.

15. B — Secure identity sets healthy boundaries.

16. B — Healing begins with honesty.

17. B — True identity is rooted in Christ.

18. B — Identity lies begin in wounding.

19. B — Truth replaces old labels.

20. B — The chapter teaches identity restoration.

CHAPTER 6 — Solutions & Explanations

1. B — Internal battles occur in the mind, heart, and spirit.

2. B — Overthinking is a mental battle.

3. B — Emotional battles reflect unprocessed pain.

4. B — Spiritual battles include confusion and doubt.

5. B — Unhealed emotions try to dominate.

6. B — Thought loops drain clarity.

7. B — Trauma teaches survival.

8. B — Spiritual disconnection is a battle sign.

9. B — Shutdown occurs under emotional overload.

10.B — Awareness and truth win internal battles.

11. A — Overthinking is a stress response.

12.B — Ignoring internal battles strengthens them.

13.B — The enemy targets the mind to disrupt destiny.

14.B — God renews the inner world.

15.B — Emotional flashbacks = unresolved trauma.

16.B — Hopelessness signals spiritual heaviness.

17.B — Identity restoration replaces lies.

18.B — Processing is required for healing.

19.B — Internal healing builds stability.

20. B — This chapter teaches how to win internal wars.

CHAPTER 7 — Solutions & Explanations

1. B — Addiction is rooted in emotional escape, not weakness.

2. B — Emotional numbing happens when the heart shuts down to avoid pain.

3. B — Unprocessed pain becomes fuel for addictive patterns.

4. B — Most addictions begin as a coping mechanism.

5. B — Codependency is an emotional addiction to people.

6. B — Avoidance behaviors hide deeper wounds.

7. B — Workaholism is a form of emotional numbing through achievement.

8. B — Overspending often fills emotional emptiness.

9. B — Pornography addiction is rooted in emotional disconnection and fantasy.

10. B — People-pleasing is bondage when identity is lost.

11. B — Addictions grow in secrecy.

12. B — Trauma bonds and addictions both create dependence.

13. B — Addiction includes loss of control.

14. B — You can't heal what you don't name.

15. B — Most escape patterns begin with overwhelm or emotional pain.

16. B — Numbing emotions disconnects a person from themselves.

17. B — Jesus heals by going to the root, not the symptom.

18. B — Hiding the behavior strengthens the chain.

19. B — Fantasy and escape avoid real emotional pain.

20. B — This chapter teaches identifying and breaking addictive escape patterns.

CHAPTER 8 — Solutions & Explanations

1. B — Abuse is about power and control.

2. B — Emotional abuse involves belittling, manipulation, and cruelty.

3. B — Victims stay due to fear, shame, or conditioning.

4. B — Abuse typically begins subtly, then escalates.

5. B — Walking on eggshells indicates emotional danger.

6. A — Gaslighting makes victims doubt their reality.

7. B — Financial control is a recognized form of abuse.

8. B — Victims often feel confused and afraid.

9. B — God's design for relationships is safety and mutual honor.

10. A — Abuse grows in silence.

11. B — Spiritual abuse misuses Scripture for control.

12. B — Physical abuse involves harm or threat.

13. B — Emotional safety means freedom to express yourself without fear.

14. B — Constant criticism is verbal abuse.

15. B — Children raised in abuse often repeat or suffer from it.

16. B — Healing begins with naming the abuse and seeking support.

17. B — God desires emotional and physical safety for His children.

18. B — Speaking truth breaks cycles of silence.

19. A — Abuse damages identity deeply.

20. B — The chapter teaches recognition and healing from abuse.

CHAPTER 9 — Solutions & Explanations

1. B — Redemption transforms brokenness into purpose.

2. B — Deliverance includes breaking soul ties, addictions, and generational chains.

3. B — God intervenes when we reach breaking points.

4. B — Restoration rebuilds everything trauma damaged.

5. A — Shame says "You are broken," not "You made a mistake."

6. B — Grace strengthens and rescues.

7. B — Soul ties are emotional and spiritual bonds.

8. B — Deliverance breaks bondage.

9. B — God uses your story to heal others.

10. B — Your ministry was birthed through deliverance.

11. B — Restoration reveals God's original identity for you

12. B — Generational healing begins with awareness and spiritual action.

13. B — Deliverance is an expression of God's love.

14. B — After deliverance, people feel lighter and clearer.

15. A — Pain redeemed becomes purpose.

16·A — God turns wounds into weapons·

17·B — Ministry is born when healing overflows to others·

18·B — Identity restoration is crucial for purpose·

19·B — Grace empowers generational freedom·

20· B — This chapter teaches redemption and release into purpose·

CHAPTER 10 — Solutions & Explanations

1· B — Soul ties are spiritual/emotional bonds, not physical ones·

2· B — Healthy soul ties come from God·

3· B — Trauma, emotional dependency, and sexual sin form unhealthy ties·

4· B — Trauma bonds include pain and attachment intertwined·

5· B — Confusion is a major sign of unhealthy soul ties·

6. B — Emotional attachment after separation indicates a tie.

7. B — Repeated intimacy strengthens spiritual ties.

8. C — God desires covenant-aligned, healthy connections.

9. B — Soul ties affect mind, emotions, and spirit.

10. B — Breaking ties requires spiritual surrender and truth.

11. B — Obsession or fixation often signals a soul tie.

12. A — Unhealthy ties feel like prisons.

13. B — Sexual intimacy forges deep spiritual ties.

14. A — Emotional confusion keeps people bound.

15. B — Breaking ties frees emotional and mental space.

16. A — Once healed, the memory becomes wisdom.

17. B — The Holy Spirit brings clarity.

18. B — Forgiveness releases emotional/spiritual grip.

19.B — Identity returns when ties break.

20. B — This chapter focuses on breaking emotional/spiritual bondage.

CHAPTER 11 — Solutions & Explanations

1. B — Dysfunction is usually learned behavior.

2. B — Emotional neglect is a common dysfunction sign.

3. B — Children learn emotions by watching parents.

4. B — Shame-based parenting harms identity.

5. B — Overprotective patterns create fear of independence.

6. B — Adults raised in dysfunction often avoid conflict.

7. B — Silent treatment teaches emotional danger.

8. B — Emotional distance repeats generationally.

9. B — Healing requires awareness and intentional change.

10.B — People repeat what feels familiar.

11. B — One healed person breaks generational patterns.

12.C — Healthy parenting requires safety and openness.

13.B — Forgiveness releases emotional bondage.

14.A — New emotional skills replace dysfunctional ones.

15.B — Childhood wounds shape intimacy issues.

16.B — Hidden dysfunction continues cycles.

17. B — Cycle-breaking requires new choices.

18.B — Feeling unheard leads to adult silence.

19.B — Healthy parenting is built on love and communication.

20. B — The chapter teaches healing dysfunctional patterns.

CHAPTER 12 — Solutions & Explanations

1. B — Royal identity is inherited through Christ.

2. B — A royal priesthood carries authority.

3. B — The enemy attacks identity to stop destiny.

4. B — Knowing identity enables authority.

5. A — Generational curses are replaced by blessings in Christ.

6. B — Redemption frees you from past definitions.

7. B — True identity produces confidence.

8. B — Walking in purpose causes you to shine, not shrink.

9. B — Believers gain access to spiritual inheritance

10. B — Trauma shapes the false self; God restores the true self.

11. B — Kingdom Ambassadors represent heaven.

12. B — Confidence flows from humility in Christ.

13. B — Walking in God's truth causes rise, not retreat.

14. B — Authority breaks cycles.

15. B — Your testimony becomes powerful when shared.

16. B — Spiritual inheritance includes healing, peace, authority.

17. B — Christ defines your identity now.

18. B — Believing God's truth activates boldness.

19. B — Accepting God's purpose begins the new story.

20. B — This chapter empowers you to walk in royal identity.

www.ingramcontent.com/pod-product-compliance
Lightning Source LLC
Chambersburg PA
CBHW051140120626
46547CB00012B/877